AFFILIATE MARKETING

For Beginners

A Step-by-Step Approach

Pal Kelly

Copyright

© 2024, Pal Kelly. All Rights Reserved.

No part of this eBook may be reproduced or transmitted in any form whatsoever, electronic, or mechanical, including photocopying, recording, or by any information storage or retrieval system without express written, dated and signed permission from the authors.

ISBN: **9798342855563**

Dedication

This book is dedicated to all the hustling affiliate marketers out there, striving to build something greater for themselves. To those who rise every day with a relentless drive to succeed in the digital world, who believe in the power of opportunity and perseverance — this is for you. May the strategies and insights shared here empower you to achieve your goals and transform your hustle into success. Keep pushing, keep learning, and never stop chasing your dreams.

Table of Contents

Copyright i
Dedication ii
Table of Contents iii
Introduction 8
Chapter 1: WHAT IS AFFILIATE MARKETING? 10
    Definition and Concept 10
    How Affiliate Marketing Works: A Simple Breakdown 11
    Popular Affiliate Networks and Programs 12
    Real-Life Example of Affiliate Marketing Success 13
    Why Affiliate Marketing is Ideal for You 14
Chapter 2: KEY TERMINOLOGIES IN AFFILIATE MARKETING 16
    Why These Terms Matter to Your Affiliate Success 16
    Key Terms Every Affiliate Marketer Should Know 17
Chapter 3: GETTING STARTED 23
    Choosing a Profitable Niche 23
    Creating a Website or Blog 28
    Required Tools and Platforms 29
Chapter 4: PROMOTING AFFILIATE PRODUCTS 33
    Affiliate Marketing Content Creation Strategies 33
    SEO for Affiliate Marketing 36
    Affiliate Marketing Email Marketing Strategies 37
Chapter 5: MAXIMIZING AFFILIATE REVENUE 41
    Building Trust with Your Audience 41
    Tracking Performance: Analytics and Conversion Rates 43
    Scaling and Optimizing Affiliate Sales 44
Chapter 6: COMMON MISTAKES TO AVOID 48
    Over-Promoting Products 48
    Not Disclosing Affiliate Links 49
    Ignoring the Importance of High-Quality Content 50
    Neglecting SEO Best Practices 51
    Choosing the Wrong Products or Programs 52
    Ignoring Analytics and Performance Tracking 52

  Overlooking Audience Engagement 53
Chapter 7: AFFILIATE MARKETING SUCCESS STORIES 55
  Pat Flynn – From Layoff to Affiliate Marketing 55
  Michelle Schroeder-Gardner 56
  Jason Stone – The Millionaire Mentor.................................57
  John Crestani..58
  Adam Enfroy – A $1 Million Blog in Two Years 59
Bonus 62
  EXPLORING AFFILIATE MARKETING IN DIFFERENT NICHES & ADVANCED TACTICS..62
  Affiliate Marketing in Different Niches................................62
  Advanced Affiliate Marketing Tactics 64
Conclusion 67
  RECAP OF KEY POINTS..67
  Encouragement for Beginners to Take Action 69
About the Author 70
Why I Wrote This Book..71
Resources...73
  Recommended Tools 73
  Recommended Platforms 74
  Further Reading..74

Introduction

Affiliate marketing is one of the most popular and accessible online business models, especially for beginners. With minimal upfront costs, no inventory to manage, and the ability to work from anywhere, it offers a perfect entry point for those looking to build an income online. But affiliate marketing isn't just about placing links on a website or sharing a product on social media—it's a powerful strategy that, when done correctly, can lead to a sustainable income and even financial freedom.

In this guide, **"Affiliate Marketing for Beginners"**, I'll take you step by step through the entire process of becoming a successful affiliate marketer. Whether you're a complete novice or have already dipped your toes into the online business world, this ebook will serve as a comprehensive resource to help you succeed. From understanding the basics of how affiliate marketing works, to selecting the right programs and promoting products effectively, this guide will equip you with everything you need to start earning money online.

You may wonder why affiliate marketing is so effective. It's because it benefits everyone involved: businesses get more customers, affiliates earn commissions, and customers find products that solve their problems. This symbiotic relationship is the core of affiliate marketing's power, and it's what makes it such an attractive model for new entrepreneurs.

By the end of this guide, you'll know how to identify profitable niches, join the best affiliate programs, create content that converts, and scale your earnings. But more importantly, you'll learn the mindset and strategies that separate the most successful affiliate marketers from the rest. So if you're ready to take control of your financial future and build an online business you're proud of, let's dive in and discover the exciting world of affiliate marketing!

Chapter 1

WHAT IS AFFILIATE MARKETING?

Definition and Concept

Affiliate marketing is a performance-based business model where you, the affiliate, earn a commission for promoting and driving sales to products or services offered by other companies. It's a win-win situation: the company gets more exposure and sales, while you receive a portion of the profit for each successful referral.

At its core, affiliate marketing works through a simple structure involving three main parties:

The Merchant (Product Owner): This is the company or individual that owns the product or service. Merchants can range from major retailers like **Amazon** to smaller niche businesses. They rely on affiliates to promote their products to a broader audience.

The Affiliate (You): Affiliates are marketers who promote the merchant's products or services. When someone clicks on your unique affiliate link and makes a purchase, you earn a commission. Whether you're blogging, running ads, or leveraging social media, you are the driving force behind generating traffic and sales for the merchant.

The Customer: The customer is the end user who purchases the product. They are the key player who drives the entire process, as no commissions are earned without their conversion.

How Affiliate Marketing Works: A Simple Breakdown

The affiliate marketing process involves a few critical steps:

Sign up for an Affiliate Program:

This is your starting point. To begin, you need to register with affiliate networks such as [Amazon Associates](), [ShareASale](), or [ClickBank](), or directly with companies that offer affiliate opportunities.

Promote the Products:

After signing up, you'll receive unique affiliate links that track your referrals. You can promote these products in various ways, such as writing blog posts, creating videos, running email campaigns, or sharing on social media.

Earn Commissions:

When a customer clicks on your affiliate link and makes a purchase, the company tracks the sale and credits you with a commission. This tracking typically uses browser cookies to ensure that the sale is attributed to you, even if the purchase happens days after the initial click.

For example, if you're part of **Amazon Associates**, you can promote anything sold on Amazon. If someone clicks your link to purchase a recommended book, you earn a percentage of the sale. You don't have to handle shipping, customer service, or refunds—everything is taken care of by the merchant. Your only responsibility is to drive traffic to their site.

Popular Affiliate Networks and Programs

Choosing the right affiliate program is essential to your success. Here are some popular affiliate networks and platforms to consider:

Amazon Associates: One of the largest and most beginner-friendly affiliate programs. You can promote millions of products from books to electronics. It's perfect for new affiliates because of its broad product range and global reach.

ShareASale: A leading affiliate marketing network with thousands of merchants across various niches, from fashion to technology. ShareASale is known for its ease of use and variety of affiliate offers.

ClickBank: ClickBank is great for digital products such as online courses, eBooks, and software. Commissions on digital products are usually higher, sometimes going up to 50-75% per sale.

CJ Affiliate: A large affiliate network that connects affiliates with top brands. If you're looking to promote well-known retailers and companies, CJ Affiliate offers excellent opportunities.

Rakuten Marketing: Another affiliate network that allows you to partner with a wide variety of merchants. Rakuten focuses on quality and premium brands.

Real-Life Example of Affiliate Marketing Success

Take **Pat Flynn** of Smart Passive Income, a well-known example of a successful affiliate marketer. He began his journey by sharing his own experiences and recommending products that he personally used and believed in. By creating valuable content around these products, he built trust with his audience, which in turn boosted his affiliate commissions. Today, Flynn earns a significant portion of his income through affiliate marketing.

Affiliate marketing is not about spamming links or making quick cash; it's about providing genuine value to your audience. By promoting products that are useful and relevant to your niche, you build trust with your followers and increase the likelihood of conversions.

Why Affiliate Marketing is Ideal for You

Low Start-up Costs:

Unlike traditional businesses, you don't need to create your own products or invest in inventory. Most affiliate programs are free to join, making it an excellent option for beginners with limited budgets.

Flexibility and Freedom:

As an affiliate marketer, you can work from anywhere with an internet connection. Whether you're running a blog, YouTube channel, or social media page, affiliate marketing allows you to earn income on your own terms.

Scalability:

With affiliate marketing, there's no limit to how much you can earn. As your audience grows, so does your potential income. You can scale up by promoting more products, expanding into new niches, or optimizing your marketing strategies.

"Affiliate marketing is not just a revenue stream — it's a bridge that connects value-driven products with eager customers. The rewards are in the relationships you build."

Chapter 2

KEY TERMINOLOGIES IN AFFILIATE MARKETING

Before diving deeper into affiliate marketing strategies, it's essential to familiarize yourself with the core terminologies that will often come up in this field. Understanding these terms will give you clarity when navigating through affiliate platforms, programs, and partnerships. Whether you're communicating with merchants, analyzing performance, or reading guides, knowing these key terms will be crucial to your success.

In this chapter, we'll define some of the most important terms in affiliate marketing, providing you with the foundational knowledge needed to make informed decisions and maximize your earnings.

Why These Terms Matter to Your Affiliate Success

Understanding these key terms will give you a solid foundation for navigating the affiliate marketing landscape. Each term represents a critical aspect of the affiliate process, from tracking performance to understanding commission structures. As you build and scale your affiliate marketing efforts, these terms will become second nature, guiding your strategies and helping you communicate effectively with merchants and networks.

Whether you're signing up for an affiliate program like **JVZoo** or **ShareASale**, or setting up tracking systems for your campaigns, these terminologies will help you avoid common pitfalls and empower you to maximize your profits.

Key Terms Every Affiliate Marketer Should Know

1. Affiliate (The Marketer)

The affiliate is you—the marketer who promotes products or services and earns a commission for successful sales or leads. Affiliates serve as the bridge between customers and merchants, using their influence, content, or traffic-driving tactics to promote and generate sales. Whether you're running a blog, managing social media channels, or leveraging email marketing, the role of the affiliate is to recommend the right products to the right audience.

2. Affiliate Link

An affiliate link is a unique URL assigned to you by a merchant or affiliate network. This link contains tracking information that identifies you as the referrer of traffic. When someone clicks on your affiliate link and makes a purchase, the merchant knows to credit you for that sale. Platforms like JVZoo, **Amazon Associates**, and **ClickBank** provide affiliate links for each product or service you choose to promote.

3. **Affiliate Network**

An affiliate network acts as a middleman between merchants and affiliates. It provides a platform where merchants can list their products, and affiliates can browse and choose which products to promote. Affiliate networks also handle tracking, reporting, and payment processing, making it easier for both merchants and affiliates to work together. Popular networks include ShareASale, **CJ Affiliate**, and **JVZoo**, which is particularly popular for digital products like software and online courses.

4. **Merchant (The Advertiser)**

The merchant is the individual or business that owns the product or service you promote. Merchants rely on affiliates to increase their sales by tapping into their networks of potential buyers. Some merchants work directly with affiliates, while others join affiliate networks to streamline the process.

5. **Commission**

The commission is the reward affiliates receive for every sale, lead, or specific action that results from their marketing efforts.

Commissions vary across programs and can be structured in several ways:

Flat Fee: A fixed amount paid per sale (e.g., $50 per sale).

Percentage: A percentage of the sale value (e.g., 10% of each sale).

For example, platforms like **JVZoo** often offer high commission rates on digital products, sometimes reaching up to 50% or more per sale, as digital products typically have low overhead costs.

6. Conversion Rate

Conversion rate refers to the percentage of visitors who take the desired action after clicking on your affiliate link. This could be making a purchase, signing up for a newsletter, or downloading a free trial. A higher conversion rate means that a greater proportion of people who click on your link are completing the desired action, which directly impacts your commissions.

Optimizing your landing pages, calls-to-action, and product messaging are all ways to improve your conversion rate.

7. Cookie

A cookie is a small piece of data stored on the user's browser when they click on your affiliate link. Cookies allow merchants to track the actions of users, even if they don't make an immediate purchase. For example, a potential customer may click your affiliate link, but delay purchasing the product until a few days later. Thanks to the cookie, you still earn a commission as long as the cookie is still active.

8. Cookie Duration

The cookie duration is the length of time a cookie remains active on a user's browser. Each affiliate program sets its own cookie duration. For example, **Amazon Associates** has a 24-hour cookie window, meaning affiliates will only get credit for purchases made within 24 hours of the click. On the other hand, programs like **JVZoo** often provide a much longer cookie duration, sometimes up to 60 or 90 days, allowing you more time to earn commissions from repeat visits.

9. Pay-Per-Sale (PPS)

This is the most common commission structure in affiliate marketing, where affiliates are paid a commission for each sale they generate. For instance, if you're promoting a product from **JVZoo**, you'll earn a percentage of the sale whenever someone purchases the product through your affiliate link.

10. Pay-Per-Click (PPC)

In a PPC model, affiliates are paid based on the number of clicks they generate, regardless of whether those clicks result in a sale. While PPC is less common than PPS in affiliate marketing, it's often used in ad campaigns through networks like **Google AdSense**.

11. Landing Page

A landing page is the destination page where potential customers are directed after clicking your affiliate link. This page is crucial in converting visitors into customers, and an optimized landing page can greatly boost your conversion rate. A well-designed landing page focuses on a single call-to-action, making it easier for visitors to take the next step.

12. EPC (Earnings Per Click)

Earnings per click (EPC) is a metric that shows how much you earn, on average, for each click on your affiliate link. It's calculated by dividing your total earnings by the number of clicks. This metric helps affiliates understand the performance of their campaigns and optimize where necessary.

Grasping the essential terms of affiliate marketing is the first step to becoming a savvy digital entrepreneur. By familiarizing yourself with concepts like conversion rates, commissions, and affiliate links, you'll be better equipped to succeed in your affiliate marketing journey.

> *"The beauty of affiliate marketing lies in its simplicity: You succeed by helping others succeed. The more value you create, the more success flows back to you."*

Chapter 3

GETTING STARTED

The affiliate marketing landscape offers a vast array of programs across numerous niches. However, not all affiliate programs are created equal. Choosing the right program is essential to your success as an affiliate marketer. A good affiliate program is one that aligns with your audience's needs, offers lucrative commissions, and provides solid support.

In this chapter, we'll explore the key factors to consider when selecting an affiliate program and how to identify the ones that will help you maximize your earnings while offering value to your audience.

Choosing a Profitable Niche

1. Identify Your Niche

Before diving into the sea of affiliate programs, it is critical to determine your niche. Most successful affiliate marketers specialize in particular areas, such as health, finance, or digital marketing. By focusing on a specific niche, you can establish authority and build trust with your audience. This trust is vital because it ensures that your audience will take your recommendations seriously and feel confident in purchasing products through your affiliate links.

For example, if your niche is digital entrepreneurship, platforms like **JVZoo** offer a wealth of products tailored to that audience, from marketing tools to online course platforms. If your audience is interested in health and wellness, affiliate programs like **ShareASale** may offer health-related products that resonate with them.

2. Research Affiliate Program Reputation

Not all affiliate programs are reputable. It's essential to research programs before signing up to ensure they are trustworthy and reliable. Look for programs that have positive reviews from other affiliates, transparent commission structures, and timely payouts. You want to avoid programs that have unclear terms or poor track records of paying affiliates on time.

Affiliate networks like **Amazon Associates** and [CJ Affiliate](#) are widely respected, while digital-focused platforms like **JVZoo** are popular among marketers in the digital products space.

3. Consider the Commission Structure

Commission rates can vary significantly across affiliate programs. Some offer a flat fee for each sale, while others provide a percentage of the total sale value. Programs like **JVZoo** and **ClickBank** often offer higher commission rates for digital products, sometimes ranging from 40% to 70%, compared to physical product-based programs like **Amazon Associates**, which offer lower commissions (often between 4% to 10%).

Another factor to consider is whether the program pays a one-time commission or offers recurring commissions. Recurring commissions can be particularly lucrative if you're promoting subscription-based products, such as membership sites or SaaS (Software as a Service) tools.

4. Look for Affiliate Support and Resources

A good affiliate program should provide you with tools and resources to succeed. This could include banners, email templates, training materials, and regular communication. Programs that offer these resources make it easier for you to promote their products effectively, saving you time on content creation and optimization.

Platforms like **JVZoo** often offer extensive resources and promotional tools for affiliates, while programs like **Bluehost** (for hosting services) provide detailed affiliate dashboards with insights into sales, clicks, and payouts.

5. Evaluate the Cookie Duration

One often-overlooked aspect of affiliate programs is the cookie duration. Cookies track the actions of users after they click your affiliate link, and the duration determines how long you're eligible for commissions. For example, **Amazon Associates** only offers a 24-hour cookie window, meaning you only earn commissions on purchases made within 24 hours of the click. On the other hand, **JVZoo** and **ShareASale** often have longer cookie durations—up to 60 or 90 days—giving you more chances to earn commissions even if the user doesn't purchase immediately.

Longer cookie durations can make a significant difference in your earnings, especially if your audience takes time to decide before making purchases.

6. Evaluate the Product's Relevance to Your Audience

The product or service you promote must align with your audience's needs. Even if a program offers high commissions, it won't matter if the product doesn't resonate with your audience. Always ask yourself, "Does this product solve a problem my audience is facing?" or "Would my audience genuinely benefit from this service?"

For example, if you're targeting digital entrepreneurs, promoting hosting services, marketing software, or tools like **JVZoo** that offer digital products could be an excellent fit. If your audience consists of stay-at-home parents, lifestyle products, and work-from-home tools might be more relevant.

7. Payment Terms and Thresholds

Before joining any affiliate program, you should review the payment terms and thresholds. Some programs pay out on a monthly basis, while others pay quarterly. Additionally, you'll want to ensure that the payment threshold (the minimum amount you need to earn before getting paid) is reasonable.

For example, **JVZoo** offers instant commission payments for many of their products, which is attractive for affiliates who prefer to be paid quickly. In contrast, platforms like **Amazon Associates** have higher payment thresholds and may take longer to disburse payments.

8. Analyze Affiliate Program Flexibility

Some affiliate programs offer flexibility in how you can promote their products. Look for programs that allow you to experiment with different promotional strategies—whether it's through blogs, social media, email campaigns, or paid advertising.

Affiliate programs that allow for creativity and flexibility will enable you to test what works best for your audience and optimize your strategies. Programs like **ClickBank** and **JVZoo** provide a lot of freedom in how you choose to promote their products.

Creating a Website or Blog

Once you've selected your affiliate programs, you need a platform where you can promote your affiliate links. The most effective way to do this is through a blog or website.

Choosing a Domain Name

Your domain name should reflect your niche and be memorable. If you're targeting digital entrepreneurs, consider a name that reflects success, growth, or innovation in that space. You can use platforms like Bluehost to purchase a domain and set up your hosting services.

Setting Up Your Website

Setting up your blog or website doesn't have to be complicated. You can start with platforms like **WordPress** (which has both free and paid options) for a user-friendly experience. WordPress allows for easy customization, offers various plugins to enhance your site, and is perfect for embedding affiliate links throughout your content.

For a more streamlined experience, you can consider hosting services like SiteGround or **Bluehost**, which also integrate well with WordPress.

Designing for Conversions

Your website design plays a significant role in how visitors engage with your content. Ensure your site is easy to navigate, mobile-friendly, and designed to showcase your affiliate offers. Include strategically placed banners, call-to-action buttons, and clear links to affiliate products.

Tools like **Thrive Architect** can help create high-converting landing pages, while **Google Analytics** can track the performance of your affiliate campaigns.

Required Tools and Platforms

Successful affiliate marketing requires the right tools to track, optimize, and scale your efforts. Here are the must-have tools for any aspiring affiliate marketer:

1. Email Marketing Software

Building an email list is essential for long-term affiliate marketing success. By capturing the contact information of your visitors, you can nurture relationships and promote products over time. Platforms like ConvertKit and **AWeber** allow you to create automated email sequences that gently guide your audience toward making a purchase.

2. Affiliate Link Tracking

Understanding which of your links are performing well is key to optimizing your strategy. Tools like **ThirstyAffiliates** help you manage and cloak affiliate links, making them look more professional while providing insights into which ones drive the most clicks and conversions.

3. SEO Tools

Search Engine Optimization (SEO) is vital for driving organic traffic to your affiliate content. Tools like **Ahrefs** or **SEMRush** help you identify the right keywords to target, track your website's performance in search rankings, and analyze your competitors.

Yoast SEO is an excellent WordPress plugin that helps optimize your blog posts to rank higher in Google searches. By optimizing your content for specific keywords, you'll attract more visitors who are likely to click your affiliate links.

4. Content Creation Tools

Creating high-quality content is at the heart of affiliate marketing. Whether you're writing blog posts, creating videos, or designing graphics, you need tools to streamline the process. **Canva** is a user-friendly platform for creating eye-catching visuals, while **Grammarly** helps ensure that your content is error-free and professional.

5. Social Media Scheduling Tools

To reach a broader audience, it's essential to promote your affiliate products on social media platforms. Tools like **Buffer** and <u>Hootsuite</u> allow you to schedule posts across multiple social networks, ensuring consistent promotion of your affiliate offers.

Choosing the right affiliate programs, creating a professional website, and utilizing essential tools are key elements to your affiliate marketing success. These foundations not only help you gain the trust of your audience but also enable you to drive higher conversions and earn more commissions.

The right affiliate program isn't just about high commissions; it's about finding the perfect match for your audience and your long-term business goals.

"Your choice of affiliate program is like the foundation of a house — get it right, and everything you build will stand strong. Choose wisely, and success will follow."

Chapter 4

PROMOTING AFFILIATE PRODUCTS

Once you've set up your website and chosen the right affiliate programs, the next important step is to learn how to promote the products effectively. The way you market your affiliate products will greatly determine how successful you are in generating sales and commissions. In this chapter, we will cover various content creation strategies, SEO optimization tips, and email marketing strategies that can boost your affiliate sales.

Affiliate Marketing Content Creation Strategies

The content you create serves as the bridge between your audience and the affiliate products you promote. The key is to create content that adds value and seamlessly incorporates your affiliate offers without being overly promotional. Below are some content creation methods you can use.

1. Blog Posts and Articles

Blog posts are the backbone of affiliate marketing content. High-quality blog posts provide helpful information, solve problems for your audience, and recommend products that align with your niche. Here are different types of blog posts you can craft:

How-To Guides: These posts teach your readers how to do something, and you can naturally incorporate affiliate products as solutions. For example, if you're in the digital marketing niche, you could write a guide like, *"How to Build an Email List in 30 Days"* and recommend ConvertKit or AWeber as email marketing tools.

Product Reviews: Reviewing products is a direct way to incorporate affiliate links. Be honest and thorough in your reviews, highlighting both the strengths and weaknesses of the product to build trust with your readers. Always embed affiliate links to the product, such as Amazon links or software like Thrive Architect.

Comparisons: Create blog posts comparing similar products, such as *"Thrive Architect vs Elementor: Which Is Better For Landing Pages?"* This type of content helps readers make informed decisions while presenting your affiliate products as viable options.

2. Video Content

Video marketing is highly engaging and can lead to more affiliate sales because people often prefer watching over reading. Platforms like YouTube and TikTok provide an excellent avenue to create videos that promote affiliate products. Here's how:

Product Demos and Tutorials: Show how a product works by creating a tutorial or demo. For instance, if you're an affiliate for [Canva](#), you could create a video on how to design graphics for social media using Canva, embedding your affiliate link in the description.

Unboxing Videos: Unboxing products and reviewing them live gives viewers a real sense of what the product is like, which can result in increased conversions.

3. Social Media Marketing

Your social media platforms are great for promoting affiliate products. Platforms like **Instagram**, **Twitter**, and **Pinterest** allow you to reach a broad audience and direct them to your website or affiliate offers. Use the following tactics:

Instagram Stories: Share engaging stories, showcasing the benefits of the products you promote, and include direct affiliate links. On Instagram, use swipe-up links if you have over 10k followers.

Pinterest: Create visually appealing pins with embedded affiliate links that drive traffic back to your blog posts or landing pages.

Facebook Groups: Share affiliate products with your community by providing recommendations and answering questions that direct them to useful products.

4. **Product Reviews and Case Studies**

Create in-depth case studies to show how you or someone else has benefited from using a particular product. Case studies can showcase real-life applications and results, helping to convert sceptical readers into buyers.

SEO for Affiliate Marketing

SEO simply means 'Search Engine Optimization. It is a critical component of affiliate marketing, as it helps drive organic traffic to your content, increasing the chances that readers will click on your affiliate links. Here are some SEO strategies to implement:

1. **Keyword Research**

Finding the right keywords is essential to rank higher on search engines like Google. Use tools like **Ahrefs** or **SEMRush** to discover keywords that have high search volume but low competition. For example, if you're writing a review on email marketing tools, you could target keywords like *"best email marketing software for small businesses"* or *"AWeber vs ConvertKit."*

2. **On-Page SEO**

Optimize your content for on-page SEO by including your primary keyword (focus keyphrase) in the following places:

- Title of the post
- Meta description (under 160 characters)
- URL
- Headers (H1, H2, H3 tags)
- Alt text for images

For instance, if you're promoting **Bluehost** in a blog post about setting up a website, ensure the keyword "best web hosting for beginners" appears in these key places.

3. **Building Backlinks**

Backlinks are one of the most powerful ways to boost your SEO rankings. Reach out to other websites in your niche and request backlinks to your content. You can also create shareable infographics and resources that other websites will want to link to.

Affiliate Marketing Email Marketing Strategies

Email marketing is one of the most powerful tools at your disposal for nurturing your audience and driving affiliate product sales. Unlike social media or SEO, which rely heavily on algorithms, email marketing allows you to communicate directly with your audience in a personalized and targeted way. With a well-crafted email strategy, you can build trust and rapport with your subscribers by consistently delivering valuable content. Over time, this relationship paves the way for introducing relevant affiliate products that meet the needs of your audience, significantly increasing the likelihood of conversions.

Moreover, email campaigns give you full control over the messaging, timing, and segmentation of your audience. Whether it's a new product launch, a review, or a special promotion, emails offer a reliable channel for delivering the right content to the right people at the right time. When done correctly, email marketing can significantly boost your affiliate income while ensuring long-term customer loyalty.

Building Your Email List

Start by offering a valuable lead magnet, such as a free ebook or a course, to encourage visitors to join your email list. Use tools like **ConvertKit** or **Mailchimp** to automate the process of collecting emails and sending out campaigns.

Creating Affiliate-Focused Email Sequences

Once someone joins your email list, guide them through a sequence of emails that provide valuable content while gradually introducing affiliate products. Your first email could be an introduction to the affiliate product, followed by subsequent emails that provide case studies, testimonials, or tutorials.

Email Promotions and Launches

In addition to regular newsletters, schedule email promotions around product launches or limited-time offers. Use email to create urgency by offering exclusive bonuses or discounts for a specific time frame.

For example, if you're promoting a software product like **AWeber**, you could send out a series of emails highlighting its features, followed by a special offer available for the next 48 hours.

Promoting affiliate products requires a combination of compelling content, smart SEO practices, and engaging email marketing strategies. By mastering these methods, you should be able to increase your affiliate sales and establish yourself as a trusted source in your niche.

> *"Promotion isn't about pushing products—it's about sharing solutions. Provide real value, and the sales will follow naturally."*

Continue reading, as we look into tracking and optimizing your performance to ensure you're getting the best possible results from your affiliate marketing efforts.

Chapter 5

MAXIMIZING AFFILIATE REVENUE

After laying the groundwork with content creation and your strategic promotion, the next step is to focus on maximizing your affiliate revenue. Achieving sustainable affiliate income goes beyond ordinary sharing of links; it involves building trust, analyzing performance, and scaling your efforts effectively. In this chapter, I'll show you how you can establish trust with your audience, use data to track performance, and implement strategies to scale and optimize your affiliate sales.

Building Trust with Your Audience

Trust is the foundation of any successful affiliate marketing strategy. Without trust, your audience is less likely to act on your recommendations, no matter how persuasive your content may be. Here's how to build and maintain that trust.

1. Transparency and Authenticity

One of the most important ways to build trust with your audience is through transparency. Always disclose your affiliate relationships. Let your readers know that if they purchase through your links, you earn a commission. Your transparency shows your honesty, and when people feel that you're upfront, they'll be more inclined to follow your recommendations.

Additionally, be authentic in your product recommendations. Promote only the products you genuinely believe in and have used or thoroughly researched. If you're promoting a product like ConvertKit, for instance, explain why you prefer it over competitors and how it has benefited your business.

2. Consistency in Content and Communication

Consistency in your content and communication builds credibility. Whether through blog posts, social media, or email, maintaining a regular content schedule shows your audience that you're reliable. Over time, this consistency will establish you as a thought leader in your niche, making your recommendations more impactful. Consistency will help you remain relevant to your audience.

For example, sending out weekly emails that provide useful tips alongside occasional affiliate recommendations can keep your audience engaged and more likely to take action on your offers.

3. Focus on Adding Value

Before promoting a product, always ask yourself how it adds value to your audience. Aim to solve a problem or fulfil a need with your recommendations. Whether it is a detailed product review, a how-to guide, or a case study, focus on educating your audience. When they see that you prioritize their needs over merely making sales, they'll be more likely to trust your advice and purchase through your links.

Tracking Performance: Analytics and Conversion Rates

In order to grow your affiliate business, it's crucial to track the performance of your efforts. Understanding what works and what doesn't will help you optimize your campaigns re-strategize and increase conversions.

1. **Using Affiliate Tracking Tools**

Most affiliate programs provide built-in tracking tools to monitor clicks, conversions, and revenue. However, for a more comprehensive view of your performance, consider using third-party tracking tools like [Google Analytics](#) or [ClickMeter](#). These tools allow you to track affiliate links, analyze traffic sources, and identify the most effective promotional strategies.

For example, Google Analytics can show you the blog posts or social media platforms that are driving the most traffic to your affiliate links. This will help you to focus your efforts on the highest-performing channels.

2. **Monitoring Conversion Rates**

Conversion rates tell you how many people clicked on your affiliate links and completed a purchase. A low conversion rate could indicate that your audience isn't connecting with the product, or you don't have a compelling call-to-action (CTA). To improve this, you can experiment with different placements for your affiliate links or create more persuasive CTAs.

3. **Split Testing (A/B Testing)**

One of the most effective ways to improve your affiliate marketing results is through split testing. A/B testing involves creating two versions of the same content with slight variations (such as a different headline, CTA, or affiliate link placement) and measuring which one performs better. Tools like <u>Thrive Optimize</u> can help you run these tests efficiently.

Scaling and Optimizing Affiliate Sales

After establishing a successful affiliate marketing strategy, the next step is to scale your efforts. Scaling simply means reaching a larger audience and optimizing your processes in order to generate more sales without exponentially increasing your workload.

1. **Expanding Your Content Channels**

Scaling your affiliate revenue requires expanding your content reach. If you've primarily been focusing on blog posts, consider diversifying your content across other channels like YouTube, podcasts, or social media. Particularly, video marketing has a high conversion rate, and creating product demos or tutorials on platforms like YouTube and TikTok can significantly boost your sales.

Additionally, repurpose your existing contents across multiple platforms. A detailed blog post can be turned into an infographic, a podcast episode, or a series of social media posts to reach different segments of your audience.

2. **Collaborating with Influencers and Guest Bloggers**

Another way to scale is by collaborating with influencers in your niche. Partnering with bloggers, podcasters, TikTokers, or YouTubers who have an established audience can expand your reach. For instance, you could write guest posts for other blogs in your niche or participate in interviews where you share your affiliate links.

3. **Automating and Outsourcing**

As your affiliate business grows, you can't do everything manually. Automation tools like **ConvertKit** and **Thrive Leads** can help you manage email sequences and lead generation. You can also outsource tasks like content writing, social media management, or graphic design to freelancers on platforms like [Fiverr](#) or [Upwork](#), allowing you to focus on strategic growth.

4. **Building an Affiliate Funnel**

Creating an automated sales funnel is a powerful way to scale affiliate marketing. *A funnel guides your audience from discovery to purchase* through a series of steps, like opt-ins, email sequences, and targeted offers. Tools like [Aweber](#), [ClickFunnels](#), or **Leadpages** can help you set up an affiliate marketing funnel that works on autopilot, converting leads into sales while you focus on other aspects of your business.

Maximizing your affiliate revenue requires a combination of building trust with your audience, tracking performance, and scaling your efforts with smart strategies. As you continue to refine your process, focus on creating valuable content, experimenting with new tactics, and consistently analyzing what is working. By applying these principles, you can transform your affiliate marketing into a sustainable and lucrative business.

"Affiliate marketing isn't a sprint, it's a marathon. Consistency, trust, and constant optimization are the secrets to long-term success."

Chapter 6

COMMON MISTAKES TO AVOID

While affiliate marketing offers great potential for generating income, there are common pitfalls that many beginners—and even experienced marketers—often fall into. These mistakes can hinder your success and damage the trust you've built with your audience. In this chapter, we'll look at the common mistakes you should avoid to build a thriving and ethical affiliate business.

1. Over-Promoting Products

One of the biggest mistakes affiliate marketers make is over-promoting products. Bombarding your audience with constant promotions can come across as spammy and insincere. When every piece of content you produce revolves around selling something, it becomes clear to your audience that your primary motive is profit, not value.

To Avoid This:

Balance your content by offering more educational and value-driven posts compared to promotional ones. Example, if you've been writing multiple product reviews in a row, switch it up with a how-to guide or a helpful tip that doesn't involve an affiliate link.

Remember, people are drawn to valuable content, not sales pitches.

Instead of pushing products in every post, adopt a strategy where you integrate product mentions naturally within your content. This way, your promotions feel like genuine recommendations rather than forced endorsements.

2. Not Disclosing Affiliate Links

Another common error is failing to disclose your affiliate relationships. Many marketers skip this step either due to ignorance or fear of losing sales. However, not disclosing affiliate links is not only unethical but also against regulations like the **Federal Trade Commission** (FTC) guidelines in the U.S.

How to Avoid:

Always be upfront with your audience by clearly disclosing that you may earn a commission if they purchase through your links. Transparency builds trust, and readers are more likely to respect and act on your recommendations when you're honest about your affiliate relationships.

For example, when recommending a product on Amazon, let your audience know that it's an affiliate link, and they'll be supporting your business at no extra cost to them.

Place this disclosure prominently in your posts, either at the beginning or before an affiliate link, to ensure readers see it. *You can also add a disclosure in your website's footer or sidebar to maintain transparency across all content.*

3. Ignoring the Importance of High-Quality Content

High-quality content is very important in any successful affiliate marketing strategy. If your content is poorly written, lacks depth, or doesn't provide real value to your audience, it won't generate the trust or engagement needed for affiliate conversions. Some marketers focus too much on driving traffic and promoting products, yet forgetting that the content itself must be valuable.

How to Avoid:

Put effort into creating comprehensive, well-researched, and engaging content. Whether it's a blog post, product review, or video, always ensure it answers your audience's questions and solves their problems. For example, when writing a review of a product like ConvertKit, don't just list its features; explain how it helps solve specific issues your audience may face, such as simplifying email marketing.

When your content is valuable, your audience will be more likely to trust your recommendations and return for more insights.

High-quality content also improves SEO, helping you rank higher and attract more traffic over time.

4. Neglecting SEO Best Practices

Search Engine Optimization (SEO) is also important for driving organic traffic to your affiliate content, yet many affiliate marketers overlook its importance. Writing content without considering SEO can limit your audience reach, reducing your chances of generating affiliate sales.

How to Avoid:
Incorporate SEO best practices into your content creation process. This includes researching relevant keywords, optimizing headlines and subheadings, and writing *meta descriptions* for your posts. Tools like **Yoast SEO** can help you optimize your blog posts for better visibility on search engines.

Also, use internal and external linking to boost your SEO and provide more value to readers. Linking to authoritative sources or relevant articles on your own blog improves your content's credibility and encourages search engines to rank your posts higher.

5. Choosing the Wrong Products or Programs

Choosing the wrong affiliate products or networks can damage your credibility and reduce your chances of earning commissions. If the products you're promoting are low-quality or don't align with your audience's needs, you will risk alienating your readers and losing trust.

How to Avoid:
Research each product or program thoroughly before recommending it. Ensure the products you promote are relevant to your audience and offer real value. Partner with reputable affiliate programs, such as JVZoo or Amazon Associates, which provide high-quality products and fair commission structures.

When you promote trusted brands and programs, you will enhance your audience's confidence in your recommendations, which will increase the likelihood of conversions.

6. Ignoring Analytics and Performance Tracking

Many affiliate marketers make the mistake of not tracking their performance. Without tracking, it's impossible to know which strategies are working and which need improvement. Ignoring analytics leads to missed opportunities for optimizing your affiliate marketing efforts.

How to Avoid:
Use tools like Google Analytics and ClickMeter to monitor your traffic, click-through rates, and conversions. Analyze which content is driving the most affiliate sales and identify patterns in your audience's behaviour. This data will help you refine your strategies and focus on the methods that generate the best results.

Regularly reviewing your performance metrics allows you to make informed decisions and optimize your affiliate marketing campaigns for better results.

7. Overlooking Audience Engagement

Many affiliate marketers focus so much on creating content and promoting products that they neglect engaging with their audience. This mistake can lead to missed opportunities for building relationships and gaining valuable feedbacks.

To Avoid This:
Always engage with your audience through comments, emails, and social media. Respond to their questions, ask for feedbacks, and make them feel valued. The more connected your audience feels to you, the more likely they are to trust your recommendations and support your affiliate offers.

Incorporate quizzes, polls, or surveys into your content to encourage interaction. For example, you could create a quiz titled

"*What's Your Ideal Online Business Model?*" to engage your readers while subtly introducing relevant affiliate products.

Therefore, avoiding these common mistakes will set you on the path to becoming a successful affiliate marketer. Focus on delivering value to your audience, building trust, and continuously optimizing your strategies. *As you learn and grow in your affiliate marketing journey, remember that success comes from long-term relationships, transparency, and high-quality content.* Keep these principles in mind, and you'll see your affiliate revenue grow steadily.

"In affiliate marketing, it's not about doing everything right — it's about learning from every misstep. Avoid the common traps, and success will find you."

Chapter 7

AFFILIATE MARKETING SUCCESS STORIES

Affiliate marketing can seem overwhelming, especially when you're just starting out. However, countless beginners have turned their affiliate ventures into thriving, profitable businesses. Learning from the journeys of those who have succeeded can provide valuable insights and motivate you to keep pushing forward. In this chapter, we'll explore real-world examples of affiliate marketers who started from scratch and achieved remarkable success, along with the *key lessons* you can apply to your own journey.

1. Pat Flynn – From Layoff to Affiliate Marketing Millionaire

Pat Flynn's journey into affiliate marketing began unexpectedly. In 2008, he was laid off from his job as an architect, and like many others in his position, he began searching for new ways to make money. That's when he discovered affiliate marketing. Through his blog, **Smart Passive Income**, Flynn started promoting products and services he used and loved. He emphasized transparency and value, and his honesty resonated with his audience.

What You Can Learn From Flynn's Story:

Transparency builds trust: Flynn always disclosed his affiliate relationships and provided honest reviews. This built a loyal audience that trusted his recommendations.

Multiple income streams: He didn't rely solely on one affiliate program but diversified his income streams across different products and services.

Value-driven content: Rather than focusing on sales, Flynn focused on providing helpful, educational content. The affiliate sales followed naturally.

2. Michelle Schroeder-Gardner – From Debt to Earning $50,000+ a Month

How She Started:

Michelle Schroeder-Gardner, the founder of [Making Sense of Cents](#), was a personal finance blogger struggling with student loan debt. To earn extra income, she began learning about affiliate marketing. She started promoting financial products, services, and courses related to personal finance. By consistently providing high-quality, value-packed content, she grew her blog into a six-figure business. Today, she makes over $50,000 per month from affiliate marketing alone.

What You Can Learn:

Choose a niche and stick to it: Michelle focused on a specific niche (personal finance) that aligned with her expertise and passion. This allowed her to establish authority and build trust within her niche.

Invest in your learning: She invested in learning how to do affiliate marketing effectively, even creating her own course, **Making Sense of Affiliate Marketing**, to help others.

Focus on consistency: Michelle's success didn't happen overnight. She built her income slowly by consistently creating valuable content and nurturing her audience.

3. Jason Stone – The Millionaire Mentor

The Journey:

Jason Stone, better known as the "[Millionaire Mentor](#)," used Instagram to launch his affiliate marketing career. Starting with zero followers, Stone strategically grew his Instagram following and began promoting affiliate products related to wealth-building, entrepreneurship, and personal development. His visual and motivational content drew millions of followers, and today he earns a significant income through both affiliate marketing and sponsored content.

What You Can Learn From Jason Stone:

Leverage social media: Stone's success highlights the power of social media, particularly Instagram, in affiliate marketing. Visual platforms can be effective tools for affiliate marketers, especially for promoting lifestyle and entrepreneurial products.

Build a personal brand: Stone created a recognizable brand as the "Millionaire Mentor," positioning himself as an authority in the space. Personal branding can help build trust and attract more followers.

Consistency in posting: He grew his audience through consistent posting and engagement, showing that active participation is essential in affiliate marketing on social media.

4. John Crestani – From Failed Businesses to Affiliate Success

His Journey:

[John Crestani](#) was struggling with various failed business ventures before he discovered affiliate marketing. He decided to dive deep into learning everything he could about the industry, eventually creating his own system to promote affiliate offers through paid advertising and online courses. Crestani's efforts paid off, and today he's a successful affiliate marketer and educator, earning millions annually through his courses and affiliate programs.

Lessons to Learn:

Don't fear failure: Crestani's story shows that *failure can be a stepping stone to success*. His persistence and willingness to learn from his mistakes were key to his success.

Paid advertising surely works: While many affiliate marketers focus on organic methods, Crestani's success came largely from paid advertising. If you have the resources, running targeted ads can dramatically boost your affiliate sales.

Offer value beyond just products: Crestani created his own affiliate marketing courses, which helped him stand out in a competitive industry. You should consider ways to provide additional value beyond just promoting products.

5. Adam Enfroy – A $1 Million Blog in Two Years

[Adam Enfroy](#) started his blog in 2019, and within just two years, he turned it into a $1 million business. He achieved this by focusing on high-quality content, SEO, and promoting relevant affiliate products and services. Enfroy's blog covers various topics, including software reviews, blogging tips, and digital marketing.

His rapid growth is a testament to the power of combining SEO with strategic affiliate partnerships.

Learn From Enfroy:

Focus on SEO: He mastered SEO early on and used it to drive massive traffic to his blog. Ranking for high-intent keywords is one of the most effective ways to generate organic traffic and affiliate sales.

High-ticket affiliate programs: Enfroy focused on promoting high-ticket affiliate programs that offered substantial commissions, allowing him to earn more from fewer sales.

Long-form, valuable content: His blog posts are lengthy, comprehensive guides that provide real value. This long-form content approach helps establish authority and attract backlinks, improving SEO performance.

The success stories of these Digital Mavins show that anyone can achieve great results in affiliate marketing with the right strategies and mindset. Whether you're leveraging social media, focusing on SEO, or diversifying income streams, there are many paths to success in affiliate marketing. By learning from these stories and applying the key lessons, you too can build a profitable affiliate marketing business.

Your journey to success starts with taking action and learning from those who have paved the way. Keep pushing forward, test different strategies, and stay committed to providing value.

"Every success story starts with someone taking the first step. Learn from those who have walked the path, and chart your own journey to greatness."

Bonus

EXPLORING AFFILIATE MARKETING IN DIFFERENT NICHES & ADVANCED TACTICS

Affiliate Marketing in Different Niches

One of the great aspects of affiliate marketing is its versatility. No matter your passion or expertise, there's likely a profitable niche waiting for you. Some of the most lucrative niches in affiliate marketing include:

Health & Wellness:

This is a massive industry with endless opportunities to promote products like supplements, fitness equipment, and online coaching programs. People are always looking for ways to improve their health, making this niche evergreen.

Personal Finance & Investing:

From credit cards to stock trading platforms, this niche specially appeals to a broad audience looking to manage their finances better. With higher payouts on products like investment services, this niche can be particularly rewarding.

Technology & Gadgets:

Tech enthusiasts are always on the hunt for the latest gadgets and software. Affiliates in this niche can promote everything from laptops and smartphones to software subscriptions and online courses.

Beauty & Fashion:

For those passionate about skincare, beauty products, or fashion, this niche offers a wide array of affiliate programs. Makeup tutorials, fashion hauls, and product reviews can generate significant affiliate income for you.

Online Business & Marketing:

Helping others start or grow their businesses online is a profitable and growing niche. Tools like web hosting services, email marketing platforms, and online courses are highly relevant here.

Each niche has its own set of products, audience behaviours, and content strategies. When choosing a niche, focus on your passion and the potential profitability of the products or services which you plan to promote.

Advanced Affiliate Marketing Tactics

Once you've mastered the basics, it's time to take your affiliate marketing game to the next level. Here are a few advanced tactics to help you increase your income:

Building Funnels:

Funnels guide your audience through a series of steps that ultimately lead to a sale. Create content that pulls users in, such as a free ebook or webinar, and gradually introduce them to affiliate products that offer value at each step. Using tools like ClickFunnels or Leadpages can make building funnels easy.

Retargeting Ads:

Not everyone will purchase a product the first time they visit your site. Retargeting ads allow you to bring visitors back by reminding them of the products they were interested in. Platforms like Facebook and Google Ads offer robust retargeting options.

Split Testing (A/B Testing):

Small changes can make a big difference. Use A/B testing to experiment with different headlines, call-to-actions, and landing page designs to see what converts better. Tools like Google Optimize or Optimizely can help with this process.

High-Ticket Affiliate Programs:

While it's tempting to go after smaller commissions from Amazon or other mass-market platforms, don't ignore high-ticket programs that offer larger payouts per sale. Think about promoting luxury products, expensive software, or high-end consulting services to make each sale more impactful.

Creating an Authority Site:

Instead of building a blog with just a few posts, invest time in creating a content-rich authority site. An authority site is a hub of information on a specific topic, packed with long-form content, videos, and infographics. The more value you provide, the more trust you'll build with your audience, leading to higher conversions over time.

These advanced tactics can help you build a more sustainable and scalable affiliate marketing business that maximizes your earnings potential. The key to success lies in continuous learning and adapting to the market. Always be prepared to evolve, and your affiliate business will thrive in the long term.

"Mastering affiliate marketing isn't just about knowledge — it's about daring to innovate in your niche and evolve with the market."

Conclusion

RECAP OF KEY POINTS

Affiliate marketing is a powerful way to build a sustainable online business. As a beginner or someone looking to scale your efforts, understanding the fundamentals and applying the right strategies will help you succeed. Here's a quick recap of what we've covered in this guide:

Understanding Affiliate Marketing: At its core, affiliate marketing is about promoting products or services in exchange for a commission. By connecting consumers with products that genuinely benefit them, you can earn income while adding value.

Why Choose Affiliate Marketing?: The low start-up costs, flexibility, and passive income potential makes affiliate marketing an attractive option for digital entrepreneurs.

Getting Started: Selecting the right affiliate programs, building a website, and utilizing essential tools are important first steps to set yourself up for success.

Promoting Affiliate Products: Content creation, SEO, and email marketing are key ways to promote products and drive traffic to your affiliate links.

Maximizing Affiliate Revenue: Build trust with your audience, track your performance, and continually optimize your strategies to increase conversions and grow your income.

Avoiding Common Mistakes: Over-promoting, failing to disclose affiliate relationships, and neglecting content quality are pitfalls to avoid in your affiliate marketing journey.

Success Stories: Real-world examples of successful affiliate marketers demonstrate that with the right approach and mindset, significant success is within reach.

In the [Bonus Chapter](), we saw how affiliate marketing can be applied across various niches, from health and tech to personal finance. We also discussed advanced tactics like retargeting ads, split testing, and building funnels to take your business to the next level.

Remember, the key to long-term success in affiliate marketing is consistency, value creation, and a genuine connection with your audience. As you continue to build your affiliate business, keep refining your approach, stay updated on trends, and always prioritize TRUST.

Encouragement for Beginners to Take Action

As you embark on your affiliate marketing journey, remember that every successful marketer started where you are now. *It's normal to feel overwhelmed or unsure at first, but the key is to take that first step.* Set small, manageable goals, invest time in **learning**, and gradually build your skills and confidence. The rewards of affiliate marketing can be substantial, but they come to those who are willing to act.

I'll invite you to follow **Mavin360 page on Facebook**, for insights, tips, and exclusive updates designed to empower you on your journey. Together, we can unlock your potential and achieve your online business dreams!

About the Author

Kelly Ifeanyi (writing as Pal Kelly), also known as **The Digital Mavin**, is a passionate blogpreneur and digital marketing enthusiast dedicated to helping individuals navigate the world of online business. With a keen understanding of the digital landscape, Kelly focuses on empowering both beginners and experienced entrepreneurs through insightful content, practical strategies, and valuable resources. He currently holds a Bachelor's Degree in Computer Science, from Delta State University, Nigeria.

As the founder of Mavin360 Digital Hub, Kelly shares expert knowledge in the make-money-online niche, specializing in affiliate marketing, digital product creation, and online entrepreneurship. With a mission to inspire and equip others for success, Kelly believes in the power of actionable insights and community support.

Through this guide, **"Affiliate Marketing for Beginners,"** Kelly aims to demystify affiliate marketing and provide readers with the tools and knowledge necessary to thrive in this lucrative field. By sharing real-world examples, proven strategies, and essential resources, he encourages readers to take the leap into affiliate marketing and embrace the opportunities that lie ahead.

Why I Wrote This Book

The opportunities for earning income online have never been greater. However, many aspiring entrepreneurs find themselves overwhelmed by the vast amount of information and strategies available. This confusion often leads to frustration and, ultimately, a reluctance to take action. As someone who has navigated the complexities of the online business world, I understand the challenges that newcomers face.

I wrote **"Affiliate Marketing for Beginners"** to bridge this gap and provide a clear, actionable roadmap for those looking to enter the world of affiliate marketing. My goal is to simplify the process by breaking it down into manageable steps and sharing practical insights based on my own experiences and successes. I believe that affiliate marketing is not just a way to make money; it's a powerful vehicle for personal and financial freedom.

This book is designed for everyone—whether you're a complete novice or someone looking to refine your skills and strategies. Each chapter is packed with valuable information, proven tactics, and real-world examples to guide you toward success. I want you to feel confident as you embark on your affiliate marketing journey, equipped with the knowledge and tools necessary to make informed decisions.

By sharing my insights, I hope to inspire you to take action, overcome your fears, and unlock the potential that affiliate marketing offers. The journey may have its ups and downs, but with the right mindset and strategies, I believe you can achieve your goals and create a thriving online business.

Thank you for joining me on this exciting adventure. I look forward to your testimonies, as you become a Digital Mavin in the online business world!

- **Pal Kelly** (Your Digital Mavin)

Resources

Here, you will find a curated list of tools, platforms, and further reading materials to help you succeed in your affiliate marketing journey.

Recommended Tools

WordPress: A versatile platform for creating blogs and websites. With numerous plugins, it can be tailored to fit your affiliate marketing needs.

Canva: A user-friendly graphic design tool that allows you to create stunning visuals for your blog posts, social media, and promotional materials.

SEMrush: An all-in-one marketing toolkit that provides keyword research, site audit, and competitive analysis to enhance your SEO efforts.

Mailchimp: An email marketing platform that allows you to build email lists, create campaigns, and track performance, helping you effectively reach your audience.

JVZoo: An affiliate marketing platform that connects you with thousands of digital products to promote, offering tools for tracking sales and managing commissions.

JVNigeria: Another affiliate marketing platform, designed basically for Nigerians, connecting sellers and affiliates.

Google Analytics: A powerful tool for tracking website traffic and user behaviour, providing insights to optimize your affiliate marketing strategy.

Recommended Platforms

Amazon Associates: One of the largest affiliate programs, offering a wide range of products to promote and earn commissions.

ClickBank: A popular platform for promoting digital products, with high commission rates and a user-friendly interface.

ShareASale: A well-established affiliate network that connects affiliates with a diverse range of merchants and products.

Rakuten Marketing: A global affiliate marketing network that offers access to a variety of brands and comprehensive reporting tools.

Further Reading

"**The Complete Guide to Affiliate Marketing on the Web**" **by Bruce C. Brown:** This book provides a thorough understanding of affiliate marketing, covering everything from selecting the right products to promoting them effectively.

The $100,000 Affiliatepreneur Success Blueprint by Dr. Ope Banwo: This book contains proven strategies for earning money online through affiliate marketing and is perfect for beginners.

"Launch: An Internet Millionaire's Secret Formula to Sell Almost Anything Online" by Jeff Walker: While not solely focused on affiliate marketing, this book provides valuable insights into launching products and strategies that can benefit affiliate marketers.

Blogs and Podcasts:

Smart Passive Income: A blog and podcast by Pat Flynn focused on online business and affiliate marketing.

Niche Pursuits: Offers valuable insights into niche marketing and affiliate strategies.

Online Courses:

Affiliate Marketing Masterclass: A comprehensive online course that covers all aspects of affiliate marketing.

Equipping yourself with the right tools and resources is essential for your success in affiliate marketing. Utilize the recommendations above to build a solid foundation for your business, enhance your skills, and stay updated on industry trends. Happy marketing!

www.ingramcontent.com/pod-product-compliance
Lightning Source LLC
Chambersburg PA
CBHW070405230526
45471CB00006B/2679